A Cat Called Panda

A Cat Called Panda

By Melanie Arora

Illustrated by Charlie Brandon-King

First published 2016 by
Guild of Master Craftsman Publications Ltd
Castle Place, 166 High Street, Lewes,
East Sussex BN7 1XU

Text © Melanie Arora, 2016
Copyright in the Work © GMC Publications Ltd, 2016.

ISBN 978 1 90898 563 7

Distributed by Publishers Group West in the United States.

A catalog record for this book is available from the British Library.

Publisher Jonathan Bailey
Production Manager Jim Bulley
Senior Project Editor Virginia Brehaut
Managing Art Editor Gilda Pacitti
Designer Andrew Humm
Typesetting James Edwards
Color origination by GMC Reprographics
Printed and bound in China.

For Anna and Rose

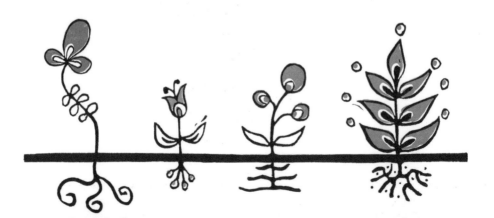

"Are you a panda?"

asked young Amanda.

"No, I'm a cat,

it's as simple as that."

"But a panda is a bear,

you don't seem to care!"

"Yes it is and I'm not,

and I don't care a jot.

For I am a cat,

it's as simple as that."

"So why is your name Panda?"

asked young Amanda.

"Now listen," said Panda, "it's simple you see.

Just like that magpie

sat in the tree,

the cows in the field,

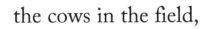

and a zebra too.

I'm black and I'm white, plus I'm fond of bamboo.

That may make me strange,

I don't care one bit.

For I am a cat and I can prove it.

My eyes are bright green,

I can see in the dark.

My whiskers are long,

and I make dogs

I can meow and purr. And have warm, soft fur.

And nine lives have I, see I don't have to try!

I am a cat,

it's as simple as that."

"Oh yes, I see!"

said the young girl with glee.

"It's clear as day is day

and night is night.

You're the same color as a panda,

black and white.

A panda-colored cat with a taste for bamboo.

Not a bear at all,

no, not you.

For you are a cat,

it's as simple as that."

"That's right," said Panda.

"And you are Amanda."

For more on Button Books, contact:
GMC Publications Ltd
Castle Place, 166 High Street, Lewes, East Sussex, BN7 1XU
United Kingdom
Tel: +44 (0)1273 488005
www.buttonbooks.co.uk